Water Invites Heaven to Sink

Water Invites Heaven to Sink

POEMS

*

by Erica Shugart

First published in 2021
Copyright © 2021 by Erica Shugart
ISBN 0 578 927367

Designed and typeset by Lucy Allen

For more information, address:
elshugart@gmail.com

for Winter

CONTENTS

Home

is across the sea,
where men smell
of the days catch.
They slam malty pints
on my table after belting
out the ancient way
of telling. Wind chimes
threaded with Donegal shells
from the deepest cerulean
dance shadows
on Mary's wall at noon.
In the back of his van
there are carpentry tools
& surfboards, & tasting
salt on young skin.
I ride his waves
until the swell
of his pupil
becomes the undertow,
until he walks into battle
against something
that needs all
his attention.
His hand, claw
of heron, reaches for my
invisible throat
& there is a soft
Connemara voice
saying,
go home.

Just in case

Ants line a path to another potted plant,
& I'm trying on my last steps
to our door. He'll be curled up
next to the boots I trip over,
his long body muted in low light,
fingers holding tight my tongue.
Prisms I hung in each window,
pillows for the cat, a garden of fruit;
women quietly make the home.
Worship a memory of him
cradling wood, heaving it into
the stove with one swoop.
The sound of the match striking,
the iron door closes shut, & then
his silk eyes & heart,
which I know, somewhat painfully,
will be there in my absence.
Love a god because flesh reminds you
of coming & going, the stinging pieces
of loss, the rotation of earth
& how winter's dark drape
closes after the fall.
The man will look outside
& won't notice blueberries
like islands on each mound,
roots learning how to reach,
growing their hands through soil.
See them rise from storms
with nothing to wear until spring,
almost drowning in the puddles
that bring flowers to their arms.
This wasn't our season,
& I'm lonely the way a woman
is awake at dawn in a house
full of sleep. But the calla lilies
I stole from the empty lot
are poking their gold dusted beaks

from white hats, & the fresh green
of springtime is calling each of us
by name.

Rewilding

Sitting behind my house,
at the edge of the bay,
the approaching yap of geese
stand my hair on end.
They sweep dotted lines
against the sky like waves
sliding to shore, dividing
& linking clans, spitting lawless
directions into the storm.
My spine stirs. The wild crafts
its survival without
signaling virtue, aligned
with the day's purpose.
Pelicans shake water from their wings,
disturbed by the sky rebels,
& water is a runway
for their triumphant departure,
yet, breaks open like breath.
Sandpipers remind me of winged gazelles,
unfazed by the geese,
dipping their lean beaks for food.
They suddenly lift off
as one loyal body of light
to evade their predator.
What do these travelers note
when car parts appear at low tide,
or when rainbow oil
lapses into their dark corners?
I'm waiting for the bay to swallow
the ground when a seal peers out at me,
safe from a virus that is keeping
me home. I call out in my best
seal voice, lightened
by the playful swirl of her body
& tilt of her head & the way
a dark cloud of pathogen conjured
this moment.

Snake

I didn't hesitate
to lift your twisted form
between my fingers,
baited by the yellow stripe
neatly painted on your back.
Did you see me fumble naked
upon the rocky cavern of your creek,
hastily tasting berries?
You move to the pulse of ground,
heart drumming at your throat
as if to answer my doubts
about our mutuality.
But you, free from an erect spine,
& me, doing my best
to stay upright against your glass eye.
Red tongue slapping at air
gets caught in the mouth
of my lover. Grass parts for
a fluid wave of muscle
& closes like a curtain
on a performer's stage —
gone to the music
of rustling leaves. A cold body
that once danced atop
a treadmill for hands
is better off without me,
& I'm left questioning
my own limbs, seduced
by the shadows that lurk
beneath my form. No
wonder the hero cut down
your tree to better
see the sky.

2:00 a.m. in Los Angeles

Sweat pants pulled over fishnets
& satin. A pair of tattered
vans & oversized corduroy coat.
In the aftermath of another
night shift, sidewalk is cool
next to him, him, & him.
They hold brass like praying,
& call beats through sideways afros.
I think about them in this smoke,
their voices pushing honey blues
swirling fickle jazz between buildings
& floating ash. Nothing left to burn
in a city of angels. A jeweled headdress
worn by *Missy Red*, blue slate eyes
hidden behind heavy lines.
The back door, then lion claw handles
closing like a vault. Day turns into night.
Customers held their feelings in drinks —
regulars weren't grateful like beggars,
& regulars weren't in love.
High heels, too thick for any ankles,
kicked the mood around like it was
worn in skin. A stage never clean.
I meant to do that when the stickiness
caught my spin.

Birth house

We lived together in the one-room cabin
he built, bed in one corner, a wood stove
in the other, kitchen with no hot water
against the north wall & a bathroom across
the field from the house & me hanging my
butt over the kitchen sink at night until I
became too pregnant, at which point he
built a bedroom & bathroom where the bed
used to be so that I could sit my butt
on the toilet after giving birth instead
of fighting the mosquitos or jumping
into the sink again where there is now a washer
& dryer so that we can use cloth diapers easily,
but nothing happens easily & the cloth
diapers never got used.

My fight

Giant leaves, sunbaked rock,
& our bodies humming at the best
swimming hole. You rest your head
across my navel like I'm a creek side pillow,
so ready to sleep your way into me.
It's over by the time I bring your mother flowers —
early apology, or my usual desperate reach?
At the equator, I'm in a turquoise dress
better for a younger version of myself
& prompt you to take my picture.
Days pass unraveling flesh in a hut.
In the valley, you're riding bikes with her
& breath leaves my chest.
That was summer, & then came the fall.
Your two wheels run slick on yellow leaves.
Walnuts I think they were,
orchards for miles & me on the ground
in a dream. Christmas in Nicaragua
reminds me I want to feel surrounded —
food & laughter spitting the air.
It's almost morning,
& you're asleep while I ride a long swell,
the full moon & morning star
branding my skin indigo.
At sunset, when a pack of wild dogs
approach us on an empty beach,
you start to run, & I pick up a stick.

Swim team

All the boys came out
       at swimming pools.

The girls knew how to slice water
       at perfect angles, then pull it past

our bodies. We walked by
       sucking in, barely breathing.

Flesh churning the cool blue,
       we lathered in the same molecules —

water, chlorine, & different types of boys:
       Olympic hopeful boys, Ivy League

groomed-for-plutocracy boys,
       waiting-outside-the-bathroom boys,

nice mix-tape boys, prom date boys.
       The girls disappeared behind doors

upstairs & came out expecting
       their keys stolen.

& there were coaches. We knew
       their apartments & stained carpets.

A scholarship to anywhere, another record set,
       & a hard-on pressed against my suit

to congratulate me,
       then hidden behind me.

Some suggested we shave it all off,
       then thanked us for not telling.

Some of us told & then
       got others to tell.

There were older college boys
       like forbidden cocktails.

A little white towel wrapped low & tight
        around his hips in a Minneapolis hotel.

I took a bus between prelims & finals,
        pierced my nose to get his attention,

then called his room for shaving cream.
        He stood at the door.

That was the first time the sound of lust
        poured out of my skin like a holy chant.

I grabbed the shaving cream
        & shut the door.

The most romantic thing

We were a river floating through
a foreign city. We were one body streaming
to the sun. At night, we pulled together
in the dance hall like winged nightly things
born in flight. Hands pressed together,
hearts aligned, a tongue and a thigh
meeting for the first time. I was spelled
by your feathers, & you were a drummer
who laughed at the empty beds we ruined.
Morning unwound our yarn, & we held hands
to the bus, windows casting light into our eyes.
The air paused when you asked me to stay,
& again when I said I couldn't
because you'd already admitted you'd
never forget the redhead from America
while I was using a bed sheet for a towel.
The driver took our picture with my last
throw-away camera. I handed you a tiny book
of Irish poems & didn't tell you there was
a flower between the pages that held
everything previously beautiful in it.
On the cover were two swans bowing
their long, silken necks into each other.

A place for foolish things

No one ever lies down in the garden
with me. No one rubs clay into my skin
after the storm. Yesterday, naked ladies

lost their petals to an autumn who envies
the color pink, & you buried our past
beneath piles of leaves.

Remember how you used to twist
inside my bath without a knife to untangle
from my hair, or the way my skin

shuttered under the rough sand
of your tongue? Each time on my knees
for you, the sting of salt overwhelmed

the room. I watched your ribs break open
like a brief door, breath rising inside
glass marbles to a wide moon

yawning & tired from spilling
the same lines up & down our coast.
We don't need to make this good.

Just let me nap you inside the ocean's
grey mouth & drink the sound
of empty crab shells crunching

bellow your feet. Suppose you laugh
on the beach again, body nourished
& returned to human, mind restored

to its quiet room. I'll hug your long waist
& bend back my neck, & you'll be smiling
at the faded horizon.

Midwife

Nothing was intended. A head
pushed out sideways, ecstasy

in between. Baby books arrived
& then collected under

her bed for a better time.
No one is confused by ambivalence.

A lot has been forgotten,
like turning off the stove,

mustard in the garden, genitals,
a season gone that never came.

Summer is flirting, dressing up
to leave its mark on our skin,

& laundry moves on the line
after drying for the third time.

You came like the first scent of spring
ready to untie winter's knot.

You hung the calm drapes inside her home,
became the eye-locked wanderer

in her galaxy. You must have seen
her militant pupils like a tribute

to the night sky when labor sung
her into the cave, ancient painting

carved on her wall. She moaned
& writhed, sunk her teeth

into a question. She flew
into the burning core of herself,

a star lost to your quiet eyes
holding her.

Post-partum

The road is silent. Feed him,
change him, walk him,
nap, repeat. Months like this,
with short moments for folding
diapers & combing hair.
Large clumps stick to my feet
in a walking trance. I say
something about love
leaving me to the wolves
& you watch me sob with his body
curled against mine.
Don't wake him
is how the days go.
Pools of milk collect inside his cheek
& we rest in a glue
of bodies forgetting their margins.
He shot into this house,
fist pressed against head
like the opening act to blood & placenta.
There are passing flirtations
& questions hung on air.
There are cries to be met
& massaged. I dreamt briefly —
a young man feeding me steak.
I eat until I wake.
We have ways to pull through
these narrow passages
like roots hoisting cement.
Outside, alder trees sprout
from each strawberry box
like resilient orphans. I craft,
& you cut through willow branches.
I write, & you sever ivy
from an apple tree, limbs
exquisitely meager & sun starved.
An offering to the last batch
of summer flies is rotting next to

some driftwood for wind chimes.
There won't be apple pie
if I can't make it through the dishes.

No one escapes an empire

In Texas, the sky reaches its long arms
above hissing insects. A rodeo
empties out & dust rolls off tires.
You sit at the bus stop where sets
of beady eyes follow you. A man
spits out his window, an engine
putters like an invitation to dance.

Judge this paternal parade
& walk your mind back to the memory
of men floating above scooters,
sunny cotton rippling their backs
soothing the wet air.
Jog into your past,
relieved by the sweat of his body,
& drag this hungry ghost empire
like a shadow braided through hair,
a subtle limp in your gait.
Fake know-how, find refuge in food eaten
on a dirt floor where a rooster
tramples ants & pitter-pattering feet
enter your dreaming. Tell yourself,
I'm safe, nothing here vast enough to conquer
& streets too intimate to be swayed.

Now you're curled up with slow
morning breath in your hair, his arm heavy
from a night of maniacal entwining,
a head full of rolling language.
What did he say? *Who cares.*
He's sleeping, & you're awake
listening to monkeys fucking on a branch
outside, watching incense crawl
its lazy arm through a makeshift door,
a relaxed spirit in heat. Tell yourself:
This is how it's okay to stay until noon.

Kids

But then, something splendid
elopes with the horizon.
The kids collect, one by one,
just like the uprising of dust
in the middle of summer,
just like thunderous hooves
against the scorched earth —
Hollywood   on fire
        think tanks   lightening struck
            Langley & Arlington   a flood.
New songs arose
from the deep dream.

Equinox

I used to have a room to think in,
sometimes on the floor

next to the bundled cat.
Now I have a slow motion of thoughts,

a waking & sleeping child to my chest,
heals sinking into the dune

where pink pompom flowers
dot the trail like childhood sweets.

Journal leads the way. A camera won't do,
but a memory of summer will.

I have rediscovered the way
everything moves in stillness.

Blood swims in spite of the mind's
soft robe, & the mind wanders

in spite of its deep anchor.
& look, lavender has been crisped

by long days, & the crystal at my window
has drunk the harvest moon.

Aloe's prickled arms are plump
& fern's edges are scorched thin.

We're leaving the way the sun
sets in summer —

low & slow, a final tremulous dip
bellow the desert.

Space

He left for the night after
I asked for space. I settled in,
peed on a stick, & watched
a plus sign grow like a hot cross bun.
He came back, & we laughed
at the idleness of wanting space.
It was clear: Within an hour,
we had evolved into a species
that could thrive on suffocation.

Then,
my flesh kneaded the dough
of a body —
cartilage, bone, eyes, & chin dimple.
There was me growing into
a tireless creature of light
with love building a neat row of trees
in my meadow. The seed kept sprouting,
the orchard needed another room.
I stretched my hands, readying the room
for the mountain outside.
I couldn't be overthrown.

Then,
childhood haunted me back
to my pink wallpaper:
Isn't there something you should be doing?
Next, my mother knocks, & I say calmly,
This is mine. & that's supposed to be
the difference. I am a good mother.
But who would choose to hold all this?

Excision

On my back, behind my heart,
I was born with a brilliant patch
of purple & red veins. I never
thought much of it until I was given
the chance to have it removed.
I held someone's hand while
a tongue of flames bubbled the surface
of my young skin. I swam underwater
in salt, goggles filled with tears,
my family coaching me. There is
a white scar in the middle
of the birth-mark now reminding me
of the paper thin blisters
& stinging white sheets.
It's funny, no one back then
asked why I should remove this part
of me. Sometimes I think the North
American condition is just like this —
loyally coaching our people along,
oh so positively prepping the next one
for salt, until some strange, uninvited
person makes a little bit of sense.

Mother's Day

It takes a village.
Are you taking care of yourself?
I have appointments. I have many appointments.
Bladder in the vagina. Do your Kegels.
It takes a village   then a smile   head turned to one side.
Say it again. Are you taking care of yourself? What about sex?
It's important for the family unit. Hold the family together.
Hold your shit together. Hold your baby, all the time. Let him cry.
Your grandma's not haunting you —
hair curled   high heels   dinner   ready for him.
You have choices. Liberated. I go for walks. Sorry, *we* go for walks. Everyday.
So he doesn't cry. Fresh air, good. Another mother. Baby in a stroller.
Big smiles. We stop. So sweet, how old? Awe, so sweet. Love the stroller.
Awe. Does he have your hair? No, it's brown. No, it's brown. Awe, so sweet.
Keep smiling. Cheeks shaking. Eye twitching. Face aching. Mouth like cotton.
Vagina like cotton. No sex. Hold it up.
Like   half the sky   or something   or other.
Hire a nanny. No money. Military budget. Pentagon polluting.
Don't mention it. They're still smiling. Look at that bow, those cupcakes.
You need them. It takes a village. Resign. Forget Yemen. You need them.
orget Venezuela. Another coup. The children starving   just like yours
n Yemen.   Oil.   Genocide.   Never mind. Keep smiling. Pursuit.
your body back. It's over there. Work it, you MILF! Body positive.
rything positive. Sex positive. Cotton vagina. Estro suppositories.
dder in vagina. More Kegels. No sleep? Sleep train.
lution.   Everywhere   solutions.
kes a village. Are you sleeping yet? Forget about Yemen. Are you
ing? It takes a village. Hire a nanny. Go to mars. Austerity. No time off.
pital bills. No time off. Baby crying. Those motherfuckers!
s   not   too   angry   now.
're fucking the mothers. They take a village. Smile.
y take a village.

When mystery leaves us

Yesterday, while you were
chopping wood, I fell
into blackberries with babe

strapped to my chest. Imagine
if you were there. You'd see me,
& pause longer than I think

any good instincts should allow.
I'd hiss something from my fire mouth.
You'd walk with your boots sinking

into mud, your limbs like a willow
branch weeping.
You'd pull me up, wipe me off & ask,

Why are you angry?

I discovered a landing place
in your soil years ago, & all mystery
fell to the floor. & anyway,

everyone likes a puzzle
not yet complete.
How will this look?

That's mainly why I'm angry —
stuck in thorny brambles,
my hands growing feline claws,

while you,
so certainly standing there
like someone to blame.

Autumn

Light moves on the north wall
for the first time since spring.

This is how the dark season
makes itself known,

hanging side-bent in the home
like an extroverted neighbor.

It spills across last night's slippers
& lands on the front window.

A coiled snake made from Indonesian
wood is there as a sort of joke,

& better than *Beware of Dog* in red letters.
The virus stole the joke

out from under this house
& leaves us perfectly shielded.

A vaccine, canning-jar shortage
& some torn up lawns for food.

A few cash-in while mothers hide
diapers in strollers.

Maybe it wasn't god enough to us.
Or in distinctly human fashion,

we made god invisible,
submerged the metaphor of her skin,

blind to her creaking redwoods,
numb to her river beds pillowing toes.

Wait for god inside another good talk,
we empathize with your pain.

Oh, how the soul of rapt innocence
wanders the endless hall, redirected

skillfully from the exit door,
never where it was yesterday

in a facility where the aged
sleep into death's hand.

Through the telescope, a distant night sky,
the dying hold our mortality anonymous,

no longer felt in the familial garden
bent over soil, praying —

You aren't obliged to survive this.

Pursuit of truth

Mid flight, two crows harass
a hawk. Imagine what the mighty

bird escapes dipping its lofty wings
like a child balancing on wind.

People gather for theatre
in the sky on a warm day in July.

A man slumbers under a bridge
trying to escape the holler in his mind.

War is a rich man's game
& someone's always selling it —

*those Russians, those Chinese,
those Iranians!*

We're spinning on a fable.
There are many hostages & no allies.

There is *awaken or die* on the wall.
Who wants to see anything as it really is?

The poet reminds you that something
is always just like something else.

But the hawk is not a playful child
& the ungracious crow is trying to survive.

Unbecoming

After machine cuts through
the brush at dusk, grasses rise
halfway to the sky like pale arms
from graves, & little invisible hearts

drum through the night
to shelter from the hawk.
Who are all these convinced
humans when not even the sun

wants a field without secrets?
They said they were going back
to the land — as quick as war,
like one rinse in a river.

Hear the rushing waters longing
for us the way life clings to each breath.
What happens to the mind
when the breath abandons its body?

See wind glide moonlight
across the glassy surface
like the ripples of your cooling skin.
Peek through the door of déjà vu

where rains once took a thousand years
to fill the river, & the protective
mountain took a thousand
more to die.

Other men

You pulled out my first grey hair
on the beach in San Francisco
& held it up like an offering.
Old enough to find this meaningful
& young enough to hold onto this like fate,
I didn't know that loving wasn't
like casting a spell. We watched
a whale head north & that night
I dreamt I was in open water
swallowing light. I moved to Ireland
for research, we wrote, & I discovered
a home in men. One drove me
across a green field to a hidden beach,
carpentry tools & surfboards
rattling the back & sheep parting
around his truck like a sacred procession.
Another stood in my kitchen
sucking lemon juice & capers
off the same fish he handed me
at the harbor that morning.
Another sat next to a peat-burning
stove in the backroom
of his art gallery feeding me
fresh bread & cheese before
everyone in the village gossiped.
Another offered his bed during my
trips to Dublin & took pictures
of us sitting against trees
in St. Stevens Green & said I didn't know
my limits, which could have
been his way of saying I didn't
have good boundaries or that
I lived too far from death.
& you were right about me
back then; always another man
in the doorway that I held open
for you. I came back, & you

canceled our plans,
& I walked to the beach carrying
sadness over my shoulders
like an old coat. A French accent,
the low sun washing his face, another
stood there holding onto his guitar.
It was his first time at the Pacific.

Her anger

Sometimes
it lands like a seed —
a garden, a new song, an hour
spent kindling July for bare legs.
Other times, a flooded dam releases
the sadness that's always beneath it;
a dark lake spilled onto the floor.
Do you see all the rare fish in there?
Do you want to swim with her,
all prune-skinned & exotic
in a puddle of her eyes
held by earth?

Sometimes it's everything
she must feel in order to ascend
like a screech owl from under his arm,
still dressed in the blue stamp of knuckles,
a nation's tongue licking his black boot.
She's banished & scrubbing
her desert mouth clean.

Tears, I know, are more befitting
the tender nape of a woman.
But like a woman, & for now,
her voice enters a room furnished
with matchboxes & ceiling fans of gasoline,
her sharp tooth striking a violin string.
See his muscle whittled down to charred
pieces of meat hanging from bone,
his black boots melted patties of rubber soles,
her bruised cheek a blushing wildfire
searing peonies.

Lost connection

I'm closest to the wild when it's injured.
A cut, then some stiches to tend.
A bruise when I abandon you most.
In the garden, as I walked up to you,
your eyes glazed over to warn
of the rattlesnake who'd just poisoned
your blood. A slow trance, a step back,
the uncoiled body slides out from under
the bush, jaw unhinged to take you head first.
You must have known what was happening,
at least instinctually, your eye meeting mine
at the last instant, the same instant I entered
your death room. Why do we want to be regarded
by the wild after we fled its call?
Your ending was the kind that haunts
a civilized thing most: Slow, yet shocking,
aware enough, yet paralyzed; flat against
a sheet, a placeless voice in the room.
You were so beautifully mastered
by death, how silly to imagine you
regarding us with anything but sympathy.

Bird striking glass

Yesterday, a bird struck my window,
a broken neck, then fell on my cat's head.

The cat, who had been slumbering below the window,
who would have rather hunted the bird himself,

rested his fangs on the fragile bed of feathers
then tossed it into the air in hopes of delighting in a kill.

I picked up the bird's limp body, held it in the palm of my hand.
The heart was no longer beating, & the body still warm.

What a perplexing combination of things! Can a being
living without the fret of time,

so close to every moment, die *suddenly*?
I put the cat in the house, bird on the ground, & the ritual began:

The ants collected, the rain rolled off its grey feathers,
& grass bent over the diminishing body.

Finally, from where I sat,
nothing too sudden anymore.

Winter

I found you in winter, a cold
morning floor, when the skeletons
of my childhood found spring.
You were there when my hips
pressed against algae in August heat
& when leaves were too slippery
to grip the old, gone stories.
You sat with me in silence when
the sky grew into the dark season
& earth flooded with rain.
There were communal dishes
& a deep voice pressing through a hall
when the white lips of calla lilies parted.
You carved flesh into my flesh,
bone into bone, a ghost-blue ache.
Lightning filled my trunk,
a dagger in my thigh.
When blood of me poured into milk
like Imbolc's first slippery ewes,
everything ugly was tossed into wicker.
Your body slid into this house,
& it would be severe in the way
I can see your moon bright face
against night's dark edge.

Where did the elders go?

Sunday morning,
tired legs upon the ottoman,
cupping warmth in cracked hands.
The daily news —
defeating *villains*
who steal *comfort* —
a story the same as
the day before.
Weekdays, there is a thin branch
for children to sleep on
& jump off when it's too late.
Saturday, there is a child
closing her eyes on the way down.
Who needs the solid ground
for a new day?
You'd drop us off
at the rest home, anyway.

Fox yard

We spend the day inching closer
after you floated through the blueberries —

a few light steps, then gone
without touching the earth.

Watch the sun sweep the hills
from behind, curves set in silhouette

on crystal mornings. Maybe you love
how light arrives along the crawl

of time at variant dips & peaks,
blasting bright fingers into your eyes.

How long to find this light in the winter?
The golden traveler in my chest,

still drunk off July, leaps through engines
on the death-strewn highway,

where ocean waves moan
from the hard pull of winter moons.

It leads me across a railroad.
You're beneath a canopy of willow,

heavy with green birth,
ears raised to those emphatic lyricists

perched inside feather coats.
Watch me roll a bloated log

close to the edge, eyes squinting
above your tail, above the heavy breath

of dew, & your wide yawn pulling me
in from the cold.

To fall for an element

I am all fire, salt feet, & tornado
circling your crown. You were a
man somewhere in there, but mostly
you swam through veins. It must
have stung to be unseen. Once,
I removed broken fingers from
your drawer, & like a child, I kept
reaching in, then left myself
in order to keep you. I laid my flesh
on your bed still in the shape of me,
a pelt in case I wanted to return.
I hovered at your ceiling fan,
watched your black pupils stretch
around me like water inviting heaven
to sink. Somehow, this seemed like love.
There is danger in teeth biting
down on liquid. There is rapture
floating to the open blue.
I don't drown anymore. I found
my skin & wore it to the porch,
loose from your wet dream, slick
as an oil spill. Years of me
shaking you onto the street
& wiping you from my brow.

If we are snuffed out tomorrow

like a fading streetlight at dawn,
we might be souls revisiting this magnificent floating rock,
awestruck by veins that flow with nuclear tar

& the last human who just slipped her skin.
We'll move ghostlike at first, taste the rotten cores of peaches
& feel some kind of reverence for the flesh we wore.

If we sound forgiving for the first time, it's because we are softened
by release, no longer marked by *I told you so.*
We spin through white museum walls & skyscraper windows,

relieved by the honesty of wind blown plastic & silence.
Dishes in kitchen sinks & lost remote controls remind us
how we were late for days spent

clocking in, holding phones & jewels
above stolen feet. *We were doing our best.*
Some of us recall our breath, the last one we took

in earth time & the people we brought through the passage
& why. Together we watch green shoots
sprout from dust, whispering, *Will we ever return?*

We witness eroding car parts & count the alchemical failings
with elder amusement — she bookmarks
where magnolias burst through sequestered minds.

We dance audacious upon lithium mines & power grids —
all our most precious death wishes, exalting in togetherness, for none of us,
anymore, carry the weight of fear or posture.

When we thirst to be needed as ancestors, some of us draw maps
to distant colonies where young stars can hear our voices float by.
In this work of a million earth years, we begin to understand

that mountains were muses, & lines of ants were guiding us
to places undiscovered. In this work of sculpting,
we rest in the calm of blue & breathe out the way of life

we were holding onto.

Sovereign

She might be the sun
instead of the one
curled beneath
the sky's black sheet.
Listen, how she speaks
without the caution
of moonlight.
Who wants laughter
to hide from the day?
She makes her own
words, strings a sentence
like straw flowers on wire
like pearls between teeth.
Don't pretend
you didn't hear her haunt
when the world was yours
& she was set on fire,
your holy ghost.
Stalk your command,
glom on to her beginning;
her wolf throat to the black night,
her pure water soaking into wheat.
Don't think she forgot
how she arrived —
into a swollen pool,
spilled upright onto sand.
Remember how she stood
without noting the cost of doing so.
Now look,
a treatment plan,
chemicals moving downstream.
See her haul a crying road
& its leathered carcasses
between her ears & hold
a child to her breast.
See her ride a bike like a bed
blooming into rain,

giant trucks from behind.
She glides
through soot puddles
parting their rainbow hunger.
Feel your strength, your fragility
by way of her, & understand,
she isn't your gift,
she isn't your ruin.

Healing

I don't dream
of being whisked away,
not even where the voices
aren't masked & the view presents
different trees,
or even imagine the smell
of fresh dough to the rising day.
I don't desire the tension
in his hand to spell *tough* & *tender*
as he lifts my hair to his nose
& rubs it across his face.
He won't drink from my well
like drowning in a desert pond
because no man ever drowned
between a woman's thighs.
I have the flesh of my shadow,
a real human in this house.
Let the sleepless hours
pass through like a familiar spirit.
A clenched jaw, a body below it.
My past spills out like afterbirth,
unwanted things flooded from
floor cracks, & I still belong.
There is a rusted playground.
We don't rise or fall back
swinging in the same breeze
or in unison. Trees aren't envious
of our soaring feet, & my skirt
isn't lifted just right for him.
I'm trying to breathe.

Resurrection

Last night you were in my dream;
how well I downplay hurt.

You were soaking your hand
to heal from the bite,

rain dabbing the kitchen window.
I waited achingly for you to notice me.

You glanced briefly, & a shadow rose
from the water & flew away.

I'm too hungry to feel grief,
& so much is lost thirsting for spring.

Another minute waits under my dress,
& the exalted pulse of leaves

slide from branches like tongues
between young lips.

The garden is a symphony —
patient, methodical, the insect prepares

to show off new skin while the bird tugs
the soaked ground for passage.

How good to remember you
touching all this treachery

with your careful hand,
childlike & ancient, losing your hat

to the tall grass & your crows feet bending
into that bright smile. We thought

we were running to a lake & found the fog
groping our thighs instead,

the car headlights beaming
until the sun rose.

We don't remember what happened next,
& you're still visiting the days

like the first trillium among redwoods,
the ray of sunlight leaves your face too hurried.

There might be a liturgy
of lighting your pages on fire & unplugging

cords while wearing a crown of marigolds.
There might be me cutting my hair

before leaving town & planting strawberries
in the shoe you left in my trunk,

still holding the fox tracks of Appalachia.
See me string all those glass beads

through your gorgeous, dirty laces.
The ceremony is never complete.

When will the dream place you
over there while I live easily

in the baffling distance
between us?

Like hope

That time I wanted to die,
bones were breaking between
the chalk of his teeth,
my soil a dense & cracked desert.
Still, some good person
left food out for me to chew.
I take my place at the table,
a candle oozes into the wood,
& smoke rises like a ghost.
I sit in the emptiness
of *what next,* then a rushing ache
like grieving something
all the way through to the birth.
Except sorrow remains
the way a newborn stays at mother's
breast, making acquaintance,
allowing for a gentler room
of the heart. Through the doorway
the bed sheet glows
from the moon, face half veiled
by the night & her whisper,
this really is difficult.
Everything old bends under
the quick death of snow
where seed scatters like mice
into the floor cracks,
my body spent & flat on the tracks
of the ones before me —
I'm like the ancestor
who hovers with a broken wing,
except I breathe easily
into the boredom
of another grey morning.
Look how rich my soil turns
when I can hear my voice
in a dark room.

New life

He studies the rested curtains,
the sun-spilled walls, checks to see
it's my body against him. His legs
kick with the certainty of his parents.
Yet, he confronts the death of us,
& joy wraps its beautiful white cloud
around a little bit of remorse.
It's supposed to be
that a child outlives the parent,
as certain as the tide
folding back into itself at shore.
But I was startled by the uncertainty
of this. The story needed my attention,
& so I held it through the night
while it gently tore open in silence,
flesh fell away from the bone of it.
There is no guarantee of another breath,
& that is the wonder I feel
when I look at him.

Meditations on matter

I sit on a riverbank of stones
moving each one aside,
digging until the ground
says *enough.* Knuckles bruised,
nail beds torn,
there is a sudden breaking away,
a slipping through to brisk air.
Is this my hand?
I peer in, & nothing but blackness.
Fear fills me, & yet
a life loving what is unsung
is my lung, liver, & heart.
If I open to this faceless sheet,
something like the rhapsodic arms
of forever will catch me.
But for now, it is perfectly good
to know the river
only by its periphery to granite,
to sit on this slab of matter
longing the firm hug of the body,
a child captured by what becomes
of this life. For now, I'm the human
dodging my existence as dust
floating in space, crouching
under a towering gateway
that echoes the names of every bird
so that wings find their way
down to its side. I'll let you be
the enchanted seeker
of leaves dipping quivering fingers
into a river, their long stems
trusting earth's firm hand.

Regenerate

If you're asking for a solution,
remember that every night
death wields red hands
through dark soil, the work
finished by morning.
In the soft folds of dawn,
eucalyptus leaves cut the air
to the calendula.

We are fortunate & risky
to love with knees to the hard ground,
elbows greased & remembering
how days once arrived well fed.
We stepped aside while the promiscuous
hum of bees took from blooms.
We remember waking
to a meadow plump
with berries in her mouth,
our muscle stretched slowly
& good sore.

You say your wrists are tied
to a trellis, that crabs left
their shells hollow,
& towers of comfrey
lean too much. But the sun rises
& the wielder's work
sweeps a thin blanket
from heavy canopies.
Cloistered children dare
to peek out amidst *green* bunkers
& sideshows, their delicate heads
pulled by the sun's emphatic light.
See them copulate hopeful
by day, joy gathering in brilliant
red & lavender hues
before night drops their seed.

Feel the ache of hot blood
letting down when they reach
for the moon,
waking & spooning the sun.

ACKNOWLEDGEMENTS

Thank you, Alex Scherbatskoy, my partner, for understanding the therapeutic nature of writing. For wanting me to write because, otherwise, I'd be a terrible person to live with. For tolerating my stealthy disappearances into my journal at times that may have been inconvenient. Your love and support are appreciated.

Zach Emilio Scherbatskoy, thank you for your presence in the new life of your nephew, for showing up almost every day like a super uncle to spend quality time with him, during which I was given another hour to write. You are a graceful offering of support and a lovely presence to the day.

Natalie Bolderston, thank you for your expert eye, precise edits, and helpful suggestions. I appreciate your encouragement and you nudging me toward the world of poetry despite my comfort with being an outlier.

Lucy Allen, thank you for doing a beautiful and amazing job of the cover and layout of this book. Collaborating with you was exciting and easeful.

Thank you to those who don't appreciate what I write about, but who still value the freedom to speak and the novelty of different perspectives. Through creative expression, may we carve space for conversation, intellect, and healing amendments to society along the way.

To Mary Oliver, who reminds me, "What blazes the trail is not necessarily pretty."

About the author

Erica Shugart is a poet and mother based in Humboldt
County, Northern California. *Water Invites Heaven To Sink*
is her first collection of poems. With a background in art
history and philosophy, she started reading and writing
poems in her late thirties, and continues to learn from the
poets she reads. She feels strongly that understanding and
opposing western imperialism and oppressive systems of
power is an important part of spirit work.